It's My State! ★ ★ ★ ★ ★

CALIFORNIA
The Golden State

Michael Burgan and William McGeveran

Cavendish Square

New York

Published in 2015 by Cavendish Square Publishing, LLC
243 5th Avenue, Suite 136, New York, NY 10016

CPSIA Compliance Information: Batch #WS14CSQ

All websites were available and accurate when this book was sent to press.

Library of Congress Cataloging-in-Publication Data
Burgan, Michael.
 California / Michael Burgan, William McGeveran. — Third edition.
     pages cm. — (It's my state!)
 Includes index.
 ISBN 978-1-62712-629-8 (hardcover) ISBN 978-1-62712-724-0 (ebook)
 1. California—Juvenile literature. I. McGeveran, William. II. Title.
 F861.3.B87 2014
 979.4—dc23
 2014006280

Editorial Director: Dean Miller
Editor, Third Edition: Nicole Sothard
Art Director: Jeffrey Talbot
Series Designer, Third Edition: Jeffrey Talbot
Layout Design, Third Edition: Erica Clendening
Production Manager: Jennifer Ryder-Talbot

Printed in the United States of America

CALIFORNIA
CONTENTS

State Flower: Golden Poppy

Golden poppies grow wild in many parts of the state. The blossoms can be yellow or orange, almost like the color of gold. The golden poppy became the official state flower in 1903.

State Tree: Redwood

Redwoods grow along the state's north and central coasts. People can see many of these huge trees in California's Redwood National Park. One redwood deep in the forest there is said to be the tallest known tree in the world. It is 378 feet (115 meters) tall. Its location is kept secret so people will not disturb it.

State Animal: Grizzly Bear

Huge grizzly bears once roamed the forests of California. As settlers arrived, the bears stood their ground. But they attacked livestock and **menaced** people. As a result, they were all gradually hunted and killed. The last grizzly in the state was killed in 1922. Yet grizzlies were named the state animal in 1953.

CALIFORNIA
POPULATION: 37,253,956

State Marine Mammal: Gray Whale

Gray whales swim along the coast of California on their way from their summer home near Alaska to a spot off the coast of Mexico. There, females give birth to calves. Adult gray whales can be more than 45 feet (14 m) long and weigh 30 to 40 tons (27 to 36 metric tons). Scientists are watching closely to ensure that these sea mammals are protected.

State Insect: Dogface Butterfly

This butterfly is found only in California. The black-and-yellow pattern on the male's wings looks like a dog's head. The female is usually all yellow with a black spot on each upper wing.

State Reptile: Desert Tortoise

Desert tortoises are relatives of the turtle. They plod through California's deserts at a speed of about 20 feet (6 m) per minute. At that rate, a tortoise needs more than four hours to travel just one mile. Desert tortoises are a threatened species. That means there is a good chance they will become endangered in the future.

Zabriskie Point is part of the Amargosa mountain range, which is located east of Death Valley in Death Valley National Park.

The Golden State

Many people see California as a special place. Pioneers with dreams of getting rich traveled there in search of gold. Today, people dream of California's sunny climate, sandy beaches, and Hollywood stars. The state also has snowcapped mountains, thick forests, broiling hot deserts, and vast fields that produce a wide variety of crops.

California is also very big. It is the third-largest state, after Alaska and Texas. Stretching along most of the nation's west coast (excluding Alaska), California is almost 800 miles (1,300 km) long and about 250 miles (400 km) wide. It has a land area of almost 156,000 square miles (400,000 sq km). It is about 150 times bigger than the smallest state, Rhode Island.

The state is divided into 58 counties. The biggest in population is Los Angeles County, which has about 9.8 million people—more than any other county in the United States. Sacramento, the state capital, is in Sacramento County in the central part of the state. Within its borders, California has a number of major geographic regions with many kinds of land, climate, plants, and animals.

Lake Tahoe's maximum depth is 1,645 feet (501 m)

California Borders

North:	Oregon
South:	Mexico
East:	Arizona Nevada
West:	Pacific Ocean

Mountains

Six different mountain regions cover just over half of California's land. The highest and largest range is the Sierra Nevada. The name is Spanish for "snowy range." Located in the eastern part of the state, the Sierra Nevada includes Mount Whitney. At 14,494 feet (4,417 m), it is the tallest peak in the United States outside Alaska. High in the Sierras is Lake Tahoe, which also extends into Nevada. It is the second-deepest freshwater lake in the United States, after Crater Lake in Oregon. In the winter, people come to Lake Tahoe and its shores to ski, snowboard, and ride toboggans. In the summer, tourists fish, hike, swim, water-ski, and sail.

In 1868, naturalist John Muir settled in California and closely studied the state's land. He called the Sierra Nevada "the most divinely beautiful of all the mountain chains I have ever seen." John Muir would later start one of the biggest environmental organizations in the world, the Sierra Club. His efforts helped preserve the Yosemite Valley, Sequoia National Park, and other areas. Many places in California are named after him, including Muir Woods and Muir Beach.

The Klamath Mountains rise in the northwest corner of California. These jagged peaks reach about 9,000 feet (2,740 m), and the slopes are covered with forests. Just east of the Klamath Mountains is the Cascade Range, which includes volcanoes. Mount Shasta, the largest of the volcanoes, and the fifth-highest peak in California, last erupted in 1786. Lassen Peak had a series of eruptions in more recent times, during 1914 through 1917. It is one of only two volcanoes in the continental United States that erupted during the 20th century. The other is Mount St. Helens in Washington State, which erupted on May 18, 1980.

The Coast Ranges start just south of the Klamath Mountains. They stretch for about 400 miles (645 km) along the Pacific Ocean. The largest freshwater lake completely within the state, Clear Lake, is located within the Coast Ranges. Southern California has two smaller ranges, the Transverse and the Peninsular. The Peninsular Range includes smaller ranges, such as the Santa Ana Mountains, San Jacinto Mountains, and Santa Rosa Mountains. The Transverse is the only mountain chain in the state that runs from east to west.

The United States Geological Survey reports that Mount Shasta will likely erupt in the future, and they rate it as a very high-threat volcano.

CALIFORNIA
COUNTY MAP

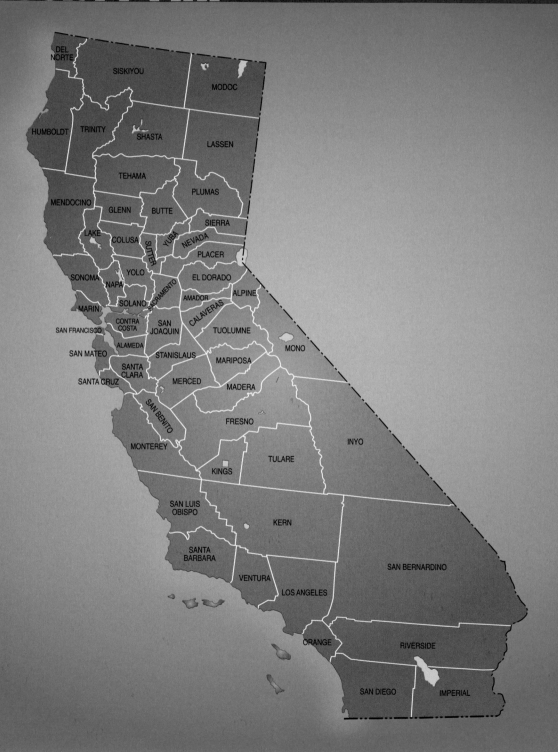

CALIFORNIA

POPULATION BY COUNTY

County	Population	County	Population	County	Population
Alameda County	1,510,271	Monterey County	415,057	Trinity County	13,786
Alpine County	1,175	Napa County	136,484	Tulare County	442,179
Amador County	38,091	Nevada County	98,764	Tuolumne County	55,365
Butte County	220,000	Orange County	3,010,232	Ventura County	823,318
Calaveras County	45,578	Placer County	348,432	Yolo County	200,849
Colusa County	21,419	Plumas County	20,007	Yuba County	72,155
Contra Costa County	1,049,025	Riverside County	2,189,641		
Del Norte County	28,610	Sacramento County	1,418,788		
El Dorado County	181,058	San Benito County	55,269		
Fresno County	930,450	San Bernardino County	2,035,210		
Glenn County	28,122	San Diego County	3,095,313		
Humboldt County	134,623	San Francisco County	805,235		
Imperial County	174,528	San Joaquin County	685,306		
Inyo County	18,546	San Luis Obispo County	269,637		
Kern County	839,631	San Mateo County	718,451		
Kings County	152,982	Santa Barbara County	423,895		
Lake County	64,665	Santa Clara County	1,781,642		
Lassen County	34,895	Santa Cruz County	262,382		
Los Angeles County	9,818,605	Shasta County	177,223		
Madera County	150,865	Sierra County	3,240		
Marin County	252,409	Siskiyou County	44,900		
Mariposa County	18,251	Solano County	413,344		
Mendocino County	87,841	Sonoma County	483,878		
Merced County	255,793	Stanislaus County	514,453		
Modoc County	9,686	Sutter County	94,737		
Mono County	14,202	Tehama County	63,463		

Source: U.S. Bureau of the Census, 2010

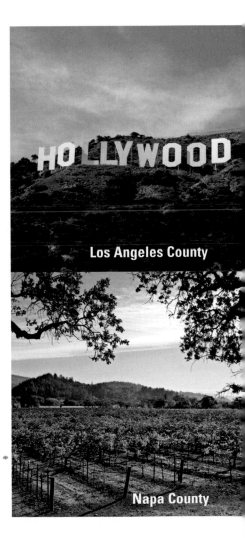

Los Angeles County

Napa County

The Sacramento Valley, part of California's Central Valley, is one of the most productive agricultural areas in the state. More than 200 crops are grown there.

The Central Valley

The Central Valley sits between the Sierra Nevada and the Coast Ranges. It covers an area of around 22,500 square miles (58,000 sq km). That is almost the size of West Virginia! Millions of years ago, the Pacific Ocean covered that part of California. Mountains rose around the water. The water trapped between the mountains later broke through the Coast Ranges and emptied into what is now known as the San Francisco Bay. Later, huge sheets of ice covered parts of California. The last ice age in the region ended more than 10,000 years ago. Lakes formed by melting ice flooded the area once again. Today, however, the center of California is a huge valley.

In the nineteenth century, the remaining lakes and swamps in the region were drained so the land could be used for farming. Water control is used to prevent rivers, such as the Sacramento and San Joaquin, from overflowing during the spring snowmelt. More recently, dams, such as the Shasta Dam, Don Pedro Dam, and the Isabella Dam, were built to do this.

The Central Valley is one of the best places on Earth for growing cotton, lettuce, tomatoes, and more than 220 other crops. Almonds, in particular, are an important crop. There are around 6,000 almond farmers in the state. They produce more than 600 million pounds (272,155,422 kg) a year, which is around 70 percent of the world's total almond supply.

Farmers rely on irrigation to water their crops. Canals and large waterways called aqueducts bring water from lakes and reservoirs to the fields. Many of them were part of the Central Valley Project, a project that began in the 1930s to provide and control water in the region.

Cosumnes River Preserve is an area in the Central Valley that is protected for its rare plant species, trees, and wildlife.

Alcatraz Island

Bodie State Historic Park

Glass Beach

1. Alcatraz Island

Alcatraz Island is a small island in San Francisco Bay. From 1934 to 1963 it was used as a maximum-security prison. Today, it is a National Park at which you can tour the prison and see the views of the city, bridges, and surrounding wildlife.

2. Bodie State Historic Park

Bodie, California is a ghost town, or deserted town, near Bridgeport. After gold was found there in 1859, Bodie's population grew to 10,000 people. However, the mines dried up and by 1932, the town was almost empty. Today visitors can explore the more than 90 buildings that are left standing.

3. Disneyland

Nicknamed "The Happiest Place on Earth," this Anaheim theme park includes rides and themed "lands." Almost 16 million people visited the park in 2012, making it the second most visited theme park in the world that year.

4. Fitzgerald Marine Reserve

Sea urchins, sea stars, mollusks, seals, crabs, and fish are just some of the animals you can see at this Moss Beach, California park. This natural wonder is a great place to learn about California's marine life in their natural habitat.

5. Glass Beach

Crashing waves of the Pacific Ocean have shaped discarded glass and pushed it onto the shore, leaving millions of pieces of colorful sea glass on the beach near Fort Bragg. Today, the area is a park, and you can walk along the shore and even collect some sea glass of your own!

CALIFORNIA

6. Golden Gate Bridge

Perhaps the most recognizable bridge in the world, the Golden Gate Bridge spans Golden Gate Strait, the entrance to San Francisco Bay from the Pacific Ocean. The 1.7-mile (2, 736 m) long bridge has an average of 38 million car crossings and 10 million visitors a year.

7. La Brea Tar Pits

The La Brea Tar Pits is an area in Los Angeles in which natural asphalt has been seeping up from the ground for tens of thousands of years. Bones from animals that got stuck in the tar were preserved in it. The Page Museum, located nearby, is dedicated to researching the bones and teaching visitors about the animals that died there.

8. Redwood National and State Parks

These parks are home to the tallest living trees in the world, redwood trees. Some redwoods can grow to be 380 feet (116 m) tall. That is taller than a 34-story building! These parks also include trails, beaches, and rivers.

9. San Diego Zoo

The San Diego Zoo is a 100-acre (40 ha) zoo that is home to more than 3,700 rare and endangered animals and more than 700,000 plants. It is located in Balboa Park. Visitors can see pandas, polar bears, rattlesnakes, alligators, and much more.

10. Yosemite National Park

Yosemite National Park, in east-central California, covers a land area of almost 1,200 square miles (3,100 sq km), much of it rugged wilderness. Yosemite is noted for its giant sequoia trees, beautiful waterfalls, and mountain peaks.

Golden Gate Bridge

La Brea Tar Pits

Yosemite National Park

When traveling through Death Valley, it is recommended that travelers have a full tank of gas and lots of water.

Hot Spot

The hottest temperature ever recorded on Earth was 134°F (57°C) on July 10, 1913 in Death Valley, California.

There are around 6 million people living in the Central Valley, and it is one of the fastest-growing regions in the state. Many of California's major cities are located in the Central Valley, including Sacramento, Fresno, Bakersfield, and Stockton.

This population growth has led to a large traffic problem between the Valley, where many people live, and major cities, such as San Francisco and Los Angeles, where many work. Some residents choose to take turns carpooling in order to reduce the number of cars on the road and relieve some of the stress of driving through the Valley every day.

Deserts

Hot, dry desert regions cover much of the southern part of the state. The Great Basin is a vast dry area that extends east of the Sierra Nevada and across the border into Nevada. It contains Death Valley. One spot in Death Valley National Park is 282 feet (86 m) below sea level—the lowest point in the United States. The valley's fascinating sand dunes and rock formations attract many visitors. The Mojave Desert, also in the Great Basin, is just south of Death Valley. South of the Mojave is the Colorado Desert, which extends into Mexico.

Within the Colorado Desert is the Imperial Valley. Although the valley receives little rainfall, it is a major center of agriculture. The All-American Canal carries water to the valley from the Colorado River, which flows along California's southeast border with Arizona.

Also in this region is the Salton Sea, which is saltier than the Pacific Ocean. The salt comes from the soil in nearby valleys. The Salton Sea formed by accident. In 1905, heavy floods caused **irrigation** canals from the Colorado River to burst, and a valley filled with water.

The Salton Sea, one of the largest lakes in the state, is part of California's Colorado Desert.

Fog is a common site to see around the Golden Gate Bridge in San Francisco. The bridge's orange color was chosen, in part, for its visibility in fog.

Climate

Temperatures and rainfall in California vary greatly from region to region. Along the southern coast, people enjoy warm, sunny weather almost all year long. Temperatures are cooler on the northern coast, which gets more rainfall. The San Francisco area is famous for its fog, which rolls in from the ocean on summer mornings and evenings. The Central Valley is hot and dry in the summer. In the winter, the temperature drops, and the air becomes humid. The mountains also have warm summers and rainy winters. Higher peaks, such as those in the Sierra Nevada, are covered with snow all winter long. The deserts are hot and dry, with little rainfall. At night, the temperature falls quickly, and winter nights can be very cold.

Life in the Wild

More than 400 species of mammals and about 600 species of birds find a home in California.

Many animals live in the deserts. Most of them avoid the sun by staying in caves or under rocks during the day. Some, such as the kit fox, are nocturnal—they hunt for food mainly at night. One animal that braves the day's powerful heat is the desert tortoise. These reptiles plod through the hills and sand looking for plants to eat. Then they return to their homes—snug holes called burrows that they have dug into the sand.

Bobcats, deer, beavers, foxes, skunks, and chipmunks are a few of the animals commonly found in California's forests. Bear, elk, and antelope live in northern and mountain areas. Sea lions and huge elephant seals live along the coast. A baby elephant seal may gain 200 pounds (about 90 kg) in less than a month!

Many kinds of wildlife live on or near the Farallon Islands, off the coast of San Francisco. A big colony of elephant seals lives there. Whales pass by, and sharks live in the waters. Scientists are studying the sharks in the wild to learn more about these skilled sea hunters.

The eight Channel Islands, off the coast of Southern California, are home to an amazing assortment of plant and animal life, including playful sea otters. An underwater forest of kelp—giant seaweeds—provides shelter for many kinds of fish, and porpoises often swim past the islands. In 1980, four of the Channel Islands, and a tiny island to the south, became a U.S. national park.

Animals in Danger

Humans can make life difficult for wildlife. Cars, power plants, and factories create air pollution. Chemicals sometimes run into rivers and streams. As cities and towns grow, people need more land for homes and businesses. All of these things can endanger, or threaten to wipe out, different kinds of plants and animals.

Several of the state's well-known birds are endangered. With a wingspan of more than 9 feet (3 m), the California condor is the largest land bird in North America. Condors live in cliffs, under big rocks, or inside holes in trees. The number of condors in the wild fell after the 1940s. Scientists then began a program to increase their numbers. More than 400 condors are alive today, compared with just 23 in 1982. In 2001, a California condor chick was born in the wild—the first one in 17 years.

Giving animals **legal** protection is one way to help save them. But some people think such laws can go too far. The effort to protect the spotted owl in Washington, Oregon, and California is one example. These birds are considered threatened. Some people want to reduce logging to protect the forests where they live. Others say this would hurt the lumber companies and take away people's jobs.

Bighorn Sheep

California Condor

California Newt

1. Bighorn Sheep

Found in California's deserts, these rock-climbing sheep get their name from their large curving horns. Some males have horns almost 3 feet (1 m) long. Bighorn sheep generally live in groups of 8 to 10.

2. Bristlecone Pine

Bristlecone pine trees grow in the mountains of central California. They are not as tall as redwoods, but they can live much longer—they are the oldest living trees. Some California bristlecone pines are close to 5,000 years old.

3. California Condor

The California condor is black with white patches under its wings, and it has a bald head. Condors eat carrion, or dead animals. They prefer large dead animals like sheep, deer, and cattle. However, condors will also eat the dead bodies of smaller animals, such as rabbits and rats.

4. California Newt

This species of newt is found only in California, in the foothills of the Sierra Nevada and along the coast. Newts are amphibians—they can live both on land and in the water. They often live beneath the underbrush on the forest floor. Every spring, they move into the water, where they breed.

5. Creosote Bush

This plant thrives in California's deserts. Its yellow flowers bloom from February to August. Many desert animals dig holes for shelter under the bush's low branches.

CALIFORNIA

 6. State Flower: Golden Poppy

The golden poppy is sometimes called the "flame flower" because of its bright color. California's Native Americans used it as food, and they used the oil from the flower as a hair moisturizer.

 7. Joshua Tree

This strange-looking tree grows 20 to 70 feet (6-21m) tall. It has long branches with spiky leaves, flowers, and fruit at their ends. Joshua Tree National Park, in southeastern California, is named for the unique tree.

 8. Mountain Lion

More than half of California is the mountain lion's habitat. Also known as cougars, mountain lions are brown, and they are 5 to 8 feet (1.5-3 m) long. They eat deer, small animals, and are known to attack small pets.

 9. Pelican

Pelicans are found along the coast of central and southern California. These birds are famous for the big baggy pouch that hangs from their beaks. A pelican takes a beakful of water and fish and holds its meal in the pouch until all the water drains out.

 10. State Tree: Redwood

The weather in northern and central California, its habitat, greatly affects the redwood's growth. In years when the weather is more foggy and wet, the redwood can grow 2 to 3 feet (61-91 cm) a year. When the weather is drier during the year, the tree can grow as little as one inch (2.5 cm).

Joshua Tree

Mountain Lion

Pelican

This photo shows a Chumash cave painting.

From the Beginning

The first humans arrived in California more than 10,000 years ago. They probably came from northern Asia to Alaska, in small boats or over a strip of land that used to connect the two continents in the north. Eventually, some of these people traveled down the Pacific Coast and settled in present-day California.

Many different Native American tribes called California their home. They included the Chumash, who paddled wooden canoes, and the Pomo, who made beautiful baskets. Most communities had only a few hundred people, but some were larger. These Native tribes usually hunted, fished, and gathered nuts and seeds for their food. There was usually enough food to go around, so most tribes were peaceful, and wars were rare.

The Spanish Arrive

Experts estimate that between 130,000 and 350,000 Native Americans were living in present-day California in the 1500s. Their lives began to change when Europeans came to California. The Spanish were the first to arrive. In 1542, João Rodrigues Cabrilho, a Portuguese sailor exploring on behalf of Spain, sailed northward from Mexico. He was the first European to explore California's coast. Explorers took the name for the area from a Spanish **fable**, in which a land called California was said to have gold and magical beasts.

English explorer Sir Francis Drake sailed along the California coast in 1579.

Nearly 40 years later, the English explorer and pirate Sir Francis Drake sailed along California's coast and landed for a time to have his ship repaired. He established friendly relations with the local Natives.

However, Europeans did not settle in California until almost 200 years later. The first Europeans to live in the region were mostly Spanish missionaries who had come to the New World to convert Native Americans to the Roman Catholic religion. In 1769, Father Junípero Serra built a mission, a settlement for carrying on his work. Named San Diego de Alcalá, it was the first of 21 missions built by the Spanish in California. The missions covered large areas of land and made many products.

Serra and other missionaries taught the Native Americans how to raise crops and cattle, ride horses, and practice trades such as carpentry and weaving. But they often treated the Native American people like children, made them give up their own traditions, and forced them to work at the **missions**.

Russian fur traders, who came down from Alaska, also lived in California for a time. In 1812, the Russians built a fort north of San Francisco. Called Fort Ross, the settlement lasted until 1841.

From Mexican to American

In 1821, Mexico won its independence from Spain. The next year, California became part of the new nation. But the people of California were used to living and working without much outside control. Mexico sent governors to rule California, but they often clashed with the Californians. The Mexican government began to close down the missions, giving the mission lands to ranchers and Spanish people who had power. Many Native Americans were forced to work for the new owners under cruel conditions.

The Santa Barbara Mission was the tenth of 21 missions built by the Spanish in California. Completed in 1786, it still stands today.

The Native People

California was inhabited long before the Europeans set foot on its soil. Many different Native American tribes lived throughout the region. There were a variety of cultures. Some of the tribes include the Chumach, the Hoopa, the Mojave, the Pomo, and the Ohlone. Each tribe had their own unique way of life that is an important part of the culture of California.

Many of the tribes travelled from place to place. Most of their houses were not meant to be permanent. They lived off the land, fishing, hunting, and gathering. Often tribes would move in search of new food. One of the many foods that many different tribes ate was acorns. Women would prepare acorns in a special process called leaching to make them ready to eat. Costal tribes would eat shellfish while tribes further inland would gather berries and nuts, and sometimes farm. Most tribes in California cared deeply for nature, and animals, rivers, mountains, and stars were often important parts of their religions.

When the first Europeans arrived in California, they did not spend much time there. However, the Spanish soon started the mission system, and set up monasteries to capture and convert any Native Americans. There were twenty-one missions in all. The missions were intended to be good for the Native people, but often treated them poorly. Land was taken away from different tribes and soon people were taken and forced to work at the missions. Many Native Americans died of European diseases including smallpox and cholera. Between the death from disease and the changes caused by the Spanish mission system, many different tribes lost their ways of life.

Fortunately, today there are many tribes in California who are dedicated to learning and connecting to their original traditions. There are so many federally recognized tribes in California that if they were listed here they would take up the whole page! A few of them are the California Valley Miwok Tribe, the Hoopa Valley Tribe, La Jolla Band of Luiseño Mission Indians of the La Jolla Reservation, the Yupiit of Andreafski, and the Redwood Valley Rancheria of Pomo Indians of California.

Spotlight on the Chumash

The Chumash people were a Native American tribe that lived, and continue to live, along the coast of southern California. Some believe the tribe may have lived there as long as 13,000 years ago.

 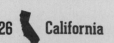

Shown here is a modern-day version of a Chumash home, the 'ap.

There were once more than 20,000 Chumash. However, when the Spanish colonized the state in the 1700s, the Chumash population declined due to the spread of disease that the Spanish brought with them. Here is a look at the Chumash culture.

Art: The Chumash drew pictographs, or symbol drawings, in caves along the California coast. It is not known what they mean; however visitors can still see some of them at the Chumash Painted Cave Historic Park in Santa Barbara.

Currency: The name *Chumash* is thought to mean "ones who make shell bead money." This is because the Chumash used beads made from snail shells as currency. The value of a bead depended on the rarity of the shell and how much time was spent making it.

Music: Music was an important part of the Chumash culture. They sang songs of joy, songs that taught children lessons about right and wrong, and songs to help cure the sick.

Games: One game that the Chumash played was very similar to modern-day floor hockey. Each team had a goal on one end of a rectangular playing field. The purpose of the game was for players to hit a small, wooden ball into the other team's goal. This game was called *shinny*.

A boy pans for gold at Marshall Gold Discovery State Historic Park on the site where gold was discovered in 1848.

In 1826, an American fur trapper named Jedediah Smith led a group of traders that reached California by crossing the Sierra Nevada. They were the first settlers to arrive by land from the east. Over time, more Americans came on wagon trains. These pioneers had heard that the area had plenty of excellent land. In 1848, they learned that it also had plenty of gold.

A Swiss pioneer named John Sutter owned land near Sacramento. In January 1848, a carpenter who was building a mill for Sutter found gold on the property. Soon people were rushing to Sutter's land in a "gold rush" that would change California forever. Meanwhile, the United States had defeated Mexico in a war that began in 1846. On February 2, 1848, the two countries signed a treaty. California and other Mexican territory (including present-day Nevada, Utah, and parts of four other states) became part of the United States.

This painting shows a wagon train crossing the Sierra Nevada in the 1800s. Many pioneers died while making the difficult trip west to California.

Making a Piñata

People who came to California from Mexico brought their culture with them, including the piñata. A piñata is a decorated container that is filled with candy and/or other treats and broken at parties. Follow these steps to make your own!

What You Need

Large paper grocery bag

Candy (in wrappers) and/or small toys

Newspaper

Hole punch

Different colored tissue paper

Safety scissors

Glue

String or cord

What to Do

- Put candy or treats into the paper bag.
- Scrunch up a piece of newspaper and put it in the bag. Repeat this until the newspaper reaches about 1 inch below the top of the bag.
- Cut strips of tissue paper 3 to 6 inches (8-15 cm) wide and long enough to wrap around the bag (the wider, the better).
- Fringe the strips by using your scissors to cut about 1/2 way up each strip, 1 to 4 inches (2.5-10 cm) apart.
- Starting at the bottom, glue the strips around the bag. Only glue the uncut part. Do not put glue on the fringe.
- When you glue on the next strip, overlap it so that the fringe ends at the top of the bottom strip's fringe.
- Repeat this until you have covered the entire bag, leaving about 1 inch (2.5 cm) free at the top.
- Punch holes all the way around the top of the bag.
- Lace a piece of string or cord around the holes, and pull it tight.
- Tie a loop in the string or cord so you can hang it.
- Cut many long strips of tissue paper and glue them to the bottom of the bag as streamers.
- You can use the piñata as a decoration or you can carefully hit it with a stick to get the candy out!

Chinese workers pan for gold in California in the mid-1850s. The gold rush attracted people from around the world to California.

A Booming New State

California's gold attracted people from all over the world. Almost 90,000 people arrived in 1849. In the years that followed, hundreds of thousands more came to California. The newcomers, often called forty-niners, hoped to get rich. A few did make a fortune, but most found nothing. Still, many thousands of them stayed in California and helped it grow.

What's a 49er?

After word spread that gold had been discovered, many people flocked to California the following year, in 1849. These hopeful prospectors were then nicknamed "49ers." This is how San Francisco's National Football League (NFL) team got its name.

In September 1850, California officially became a U.S. state. It was admitted as a "free" state, where people could not own or trade slaves. At that time, San Francisco was becoming California's most important city. It had a good harbor and was near the hills where gold

A Central Pacific Railroad train winds through the Yosemite Valley in the 1860s. The expansion of railroads in the 1860s connected California with the rest of the country.

had been found. Prior to the gold rush, the city had a tiny population. By 1852, more than 35,000 people lived in San Francisco. The forty-niners needed food, clothing, and places to sleep, so people who were not mining for gold found work supplying the miners.

The newcomers included Chinese workers, a new wave of Mexicans, and free African Americans. Some African Americans used their wealth from mining gold to buy the freedom of relatives held as slaves in the South.

Land of Riches

The gold rush did not go on forever, but California kept growing. In 1869, a transcontinental railroad linked California with the eastern United States. The railroad made it easier for people and goods to reach the state. The business leaders who helped bring about the building of the rail lines became millionaires. However, the Chinese **immigrants** who did much of the actual labor of building the railroads did not get much money for their hard work.

Chinese employees received $27 to $30 a month, which did not include the cost of food and a place to stay. Immigrants from Ireland and other "white" workers, though, were paid $35 per month, which did include the cost of a place to stay. The work was dangerous, and much of it was done with hand tools. Employees worked 12 hours a day, six days a week.

California's farmland provided other jobs. Because many areas did not have enough rain to raise crops, the state began a series of irrigation projects to bring water to dry land. By the end of the nineteenth century, land was cheap and many people had the opportunity to own farms.

California's rich farmland attracted workers from all over the world.

Los Angeles

San Diego

San Francisco

1. Los Angeles: population 3,792,621

L.A. is best known for Hollywood, a district within the city. Many TV shows and movies are made there. Famous L.A. landmarks include the Hollywood Walk of Fame, the Griffith Observatory, and nearby Venice Beach.

2. San Diego: population 1,307,402

Beautiful weather, gorgeous beaches, and outdoor activities are just some of the reasons more than a million people call San Diego home. Located just north of the Mexico border, residents and visitors enjoy biking, hiking, surfing, and more.

3. San Jose: population 945,942

San Jose sits in an area nicknamed "**Silicon** Valley." This term refers to the large number of silicon–chip manufacturers that were once located there. Now, many of the world's biggest technology companies are headquartered in or near San Jose.

4. San Francisco: population 805,235

Known as "The City by the Bay," San Francisco is a city full of sites to see and things to do. Some of the most famous landmarks in California are right there. You can ride a cable car, explore Golden Gate Park, or watch the sea lions at Pier 39!

5. Fresno: population 494,665

Fresno County, in central California, is the number one agricultural producer in the United States. The area is known for its abundant produce. Fresno is also close to three major national parks: Yosemite, Sequoia, and Kings Canyon National Parks.

CALIFORNIA

6. Sacramento: population 466,488

Sacramento is the capital of California. Gold was discovered around 50 miles (80 km) northeast of the city, which led to the California Gold Rush. Sacramento quickly grew in size and population. Today, visitors can enjoy the capital's parks, museums, and riverfront.

7. Long Beach: population 462,257

Long Beach is a community located between Los Angeles and Orange County. The Port of Long Beach is one of the largest shipping ports in the world. The city is also home to the *RMS Queen Mary,* a retired ship that once transported troops during WWII. Today, you can tour the ship.

8. Oakland: population 360,724

Oakland sits across the bay from San Francisco. It is home to three professional sports teams: the Oakland Athletics (baseball), Oakland Raiders (football), and the Golden State Warriors (basketball). There is also a large artist community there, along with parks and a lakefront (Lake Merritt).

9. Bakersfield: population 347,483

Bakersfield is the oil-producing capital of California. "The Bakersfield Sound," a twang-y way of playing the steel guitar, was made famous by country singers Merle Haggard and Buck Owens during the 1950s.

10. Anaheim: population 336,265

Anaheim, located outside of Los Angeles, is best known for being the home of one of the most visited tourist attractions in the world: Disneyland Resort.

Sacramento

Long Beach

Bakersfield

The 1906 earthquake and the fires it caused left much of San Francisco in ruins.

The Big Quake

On Wednesday, April 18, 1906, at about 5 a.m., an earthquake started off the coast of San Francisco and moved into the city. It lasted only about a minute. But buildings crumbled, streets cracked apart, and **debris** flew everywhere. Gas lines broke, causing fires that raged out of control for days. In the end, more than 3,000 people were killed in and near the city. Many more were injured or left homeless. But aid poured in from far and wide, and before long the determined people of San Francisco rebuilt their city.

Lights, Camera, Action!

In the early 20th century, the movie industry was born. Filmmakers realized that the warm climate and open space of southern California made it the perfect spot to make movies. The film industry grew up in an area of Los Angeles called Hollywood. To many, it seemed like a magical place, where dreams came to life on the screen. California drew thousands of people looking for work in the movie industry. Hollywood is still the movie capital of the world.

In Their Own Words

"The ground seemed to twist under us like a top while it jerked this way and that, up and down and every way."

—A San Francisco police officer who was on patrol during the 1906 earthquake

Depression and War

In the 1920s, California and the rest of the United States had a strong economy. After 1929, however, the country faced difficult times. During the Great Depression, many banks failed and businesses closed. People lost the money they had saved in the banks, and millions of workers lost their jobs. During the 1930s, years of drought and terrible dust storms destroyed farms and homes across the Great Plains. Hundreds of thousands of people from the region, which became known as the Dust Bowl, packed up and moved to California. They were attracted by the mild climate and long growing season. Many were treated poorly by Californians, however, and scraped by in low-paying jobs picking cotton or fruit.

In the 1940s, World War II helped pull California and the rest of the country out of the Depression. The U.S. government spent billions of dollars to make ships, planes, weapons, and supplies. The state was a center for those industries, and jobs in the factories and shipyards lured more people to California.

Charlie Chaplin was one of the first big Hollywood movie stars. This photo shows a scene from the 1925 film *The Gold Rush*.

Two hippies walk through Golden Gate Park in San Francisco in 1969.

After the War

After World War II, companies that made weapons, ships, and planes continued to get work from the government. People were drawn to the state's warm weather. Many thought California had an easygoing, "laid-back" lifestyle. By the mid–1960s, more people lived in California than in any other state.

For some people, California was a place where they could dress, speak, and act differently from the typical American. In the 1950s, poets such as Allen Ginsberg and writers such as Jack Kerouac flocked to San Francisco and wrote about life as they saw it. These writers and others became known as "beatniks."

In the 1960s, California was the center of a so-called youth movement. The interests of teenagers and young adults shaped music and film. The Beach Boys and other California groups sang about the beach, surfing, dating, and cars.

During the 1960s, the United States became involved in a war in Vietnam, a country in Southeast Asia. Many Americans opposed the war and organized protests. At the University of California at Berkeley, students staged sits-ins in school buildings and called for changes in running the university. Many were arrested in **confrontations** with police.

Meanwhile, in San Francisco, "hippies" found a home. Many wore sandals or went barefoot and grew their hair long. Some took illegal drugs and lived on the street.

Silicon Valley

During the 20th century, the Santa Clara Valley, south of San Francisco Bay, developed as a center for technology. The area has become known as Silicon Valley, because silicon is commonly used to make the chips that power computers. Hewlett–Packard was started there in the late 1930s. Intel arrived in the late 1960s. In 1976, Steve Jobs and his friend Steve Wozniak founded Apple, an important computer company. In the 1990s, Yahoo! and Google were among the many Internet companies that started in the valley. Today, industries that produce computers and computer software, along with Internet service industries, are key parts of the state's economy.

The Enchanted Hill

Hearst Castle is a home that was built for newspaper publisher William Randolph Hearst along the Pacific Coast, starting in 1919. It has 165 rooms, 38 bedrooms, 61 bathrooms, 14 sitting rooms, a kitchen, a movie theater, 2 libraries, a billiard room, a dining hall, an assembly hall, 41 fireplaces, and 127 acres [51 ha] of gardens. Hearst nicknamed the hill it sits on "La Cuesta Encantada," which means "The Enchanted Hill" in Spanish.

Apple cofounder Steve Jobs unveils a new Apple product in 2010.

Apple's headquarters are located in Cupertino, California, in Silicon Valley.

I'll Take a Ticket!

The Country Store in Baker, California has sold more winning California State Lottery tickets than any other place in the state.

By 2000, the computer boom was slowing. Some people who **invested** in high-tech companies in Silicon Valley lost much of their money, and many workers in Silicon Valley lost their jobs. Those losses meant that the state government got less money from taxes. At the same time, California's population was growing fast, and the government was spending more and more money on services. California also faced a big energy crunch. As the population increased, so did the demand for electricity, but new power plants had not been built. As electricity prices rose, some businesses had to shut down because of high energy costs.

Under California law, an elected official can be removed from office and replaced by someone else in a special "recall" election. That happened in October 2003, when voters removed Governor Gray Davis and replaced him with Arnold Schwarzenegger, a former body builder and action-film star who had become active in politics.

Governor Schwarzenegger arrives at a rally to raise money for U.S. military troops.

Even with a new governor, the state still had money problems. In 2008, the economy of the whole country took a downturn. In 2009, California's governor and legislature missed a deadline for approving a new **budget**. The government briefly ran out of money and had to issue IOUs (signed promises) to people who were supposed to receive checks from the state. A budget was finally adopted, and the state began to pay up. But the new budget called for big cuts in education and other services. The government still had worries about making ends meet. Governor Schwarzenegger called on the people of California to pull together and make the sacrifices needed to help solve the state's financial problems.

Governor Jerry Brown and President Barack Obama talk to a California farmer about the state's drought that began in 2013.

10 KEY DATES IN STATE HISTORY

1. September 1542
João Rodrigues Cabrilho explores the California coast. He becomes the first European to set foot in what is now California.

2. January 24, 1848
Gold is found at Sutter's Mill, and the Gold Rush begins. A few weeks later, the United States receives California from Mexico.

3. September 9, 1850
Californians sought statehood and, after a heated debate about slavery, California enters the Union as a free, non-slavery state. California is the 31st state.

4. May 10, 1869
The first transcontinental railroad is completed, linking California with the eastern United States. One of the last spikes that completed the railroad is on display at Sacramento's California State Railroad Museum.

5. April 18, 1906
An earthquake and fires destroy much of San Francisco. It is estimated that 80 percent of the city was demolished.

6. 1970
The opening of the Palo Alto Research Center leads to the development of Silicon Valley.

7. October 17, 1989
A magnitude 6.9 earthquake hits the San Francisco and Monterey Bay regions near Loma Prieta Peak in the Santa Cruz Mountains. The earthquake kills more than 60 people and injures more than 3,700.

8. October 7, 2003
Californians vote to remove Governor Gray Davis from office and elect Arnold Schwarzenegger in his place. He goes on to serve a second term as governor.

9. October 5, 2011
Steve Jobs, cofounder of Apple, Inc., dies at his home in Palo Alto after a long battle with cancer.

10. February 24, 2014
Senator Ron Calderon surrenders to police after being charged with accepting money for legislative favors, along with other illegal activities. He pleads not guilty.

A man performs acrobatic jumps on Venice Beach, near Los Angeles. Venice Beach is known for its unique artists, vendors, and street performers.

The People

From its earliest beginnings, California has been home to a mix of different peoples. The Native American groups had differences in language and culture. They were joined—and to a large extent pushed aside—by Spanish settlers from the south and English-speaking pioneers from the east. The gold rush that started in 1848 drew a large wave of people to California from all corners of the world. After the gold rush, the state continued to attract people to work in its mines, railroads, fields, shipyards, and factories. Today, people from countries far and wide live in California and work in its service and high-tech industries.

At times, people from different groups have clashed. Native Americans, Hispanics, Asians, and African Americans have all suffered from injustice and discrimination. At the same time, all these groups have added to the culture of California and helped build the state into what it is today.

Cars and trucks choke Interstate 405 during rush hour in Los Angeles.

The California Melting Pot

Some 27 percent of Californians, more than one out of every four, are foreign-born. That is the highest percentage for any state. New York ranks second, with about 22 percent of its people born in other countries. Many other Californians have parents who were immigrants.

Counting Californians

As of 2010, California had more than 37 million people—by far the largest population of any state. It had about 12 million more people than the second-most populous state, Texas. California is also the most diverse state in the country. Well over one-third of all Californians are Hispanic or Latino. That means that they or their ancestors came from Mexico or another Spanish-speaking country. About one of every eight Californians is Asian, and about one of fifteen is African American.

Although California has a lot of wide-open spaces, most of the people live clustered together in suburbs and cities. The Los Angeles–Long Beach–Anaheim metropolitan area has more than 12 million people, almost one-third of the state's total population.

As of 2010, Los Angeles alone had more than 3.7 million people. It is the biggest city in California and the second biggest in the United States, behind New York City. San Diego is the second-largest California city, with 1.3 million people. It is followed by San Jose, with 945,000, and San Francisco, with 805,000. Also among the top 50 U.S. cities in population are Fresno, Long Beach, Sacramento (California's capital), and Oakland (located next to San Francisco).

Though California has many cities with 100,000 people or more, small towns in the desert and in the mountains have only a few hundred residents. These places can be hours away from big cities, with only a few roads and stores. Northern California, between Sacramento and Oregon, is a region the size of New York State, but it has only about 5 percent of California's residents. People say it is cheaper to live there than in the rest of California.

San Luis Obispo is a small city located halfway between Los Angeles and San Francisco. Author and researcher Dan Buettner named it the "Happiest City in America" in 2010.

10 KEY PEOPLE

Jessica Alba

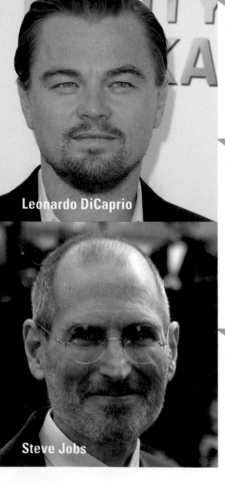

Leonardo DiCaprio

Steve Jobs

1. Jessica Alba

Born in Pomona, Jessica Alba is a Mexican-American actress who is best known for her roles in *Dark Angel* and *Fantastic Four: Rise of the Silver Surfer*.

2. Tom Brady

Tom Brady is a famous quarterback for the New England Patriots. He was born and raised in San Mateo. Brady has led the team to three Super Bowl championships and has been named Most Valuable Player in the National Football League (NFL) three times.

3. Leonardo DiCaprio

Born in 1974 in Los Angeles, Leonardo DiCaprio started out as a child actor. He became world famous in 1997 when he starred in *Titanic*. By 2014, he had been nominated for four Academy Awards—the top award for films.

4. Steve Jobs

As a child, Steve Jobs spent time in his father's garage in Mountain View, California working on electronics. Years later, Jobs became the cofounder of Apple, Inc., one of the largest corporations in the world. Jobs is known as one of the greatest innovators in the world of computers, phones, and other personal electronics.

5. Jack London

Jack London is the author of *The Call of the Wild* and *White Fang*, two of the most popular novels of the early 20th Century. Born John Griffith Chaney in San Francisco, London spent time in Alaska searching for gold before coming back to California. His experiences in both places inspired many of his stories.

6. Ellen Ochoa

Born in 1958 in Los Angeles, Ellen Ochoa studied engineering at Stanford University. She applied to the U.S. astronaut-training program and was selected in 1990. In 1993, Ochoa became the first Hispanic woman to travel into space.

7. Nancy Pelosi

Nancy Pelosi was born in 1940 in Baltimore, Maryland, but moved to San Francisco after she got married. She won her first election to the U.S. House of Representatives in 1987. In 2007, she became the first woman to be Speaker of the House.

8. Antonio Villaraigosa

Antonio Villaraigosa was born in East Los Angeles in 1953. He was elected to the State Assembly in 1994 and became Speaker four years later. In 2005, Villaraigosa became the first Hispanic mayor of Los Angeles in more than 100 years.

9. Serena and Venus Williams

The Williams sisters grew up in Compton. Their father taught them how to play tennis. As teenagers, the sisters rose to the top. They have won more than a dozen grand slam titles as partners. Through 2013, Serena had won 17 singles championships—eight more than her big sister.

10. Tiger Woods

Eldrick Tont "Tiger" Woods was born in Cypress. His father began teaching Woods how to play golf at the age of two! In 1997, Woods won the Masters Championship, becoming the first African American to win the title. Since then, Woods has become one of the highest-earning and greatest golfers in history.

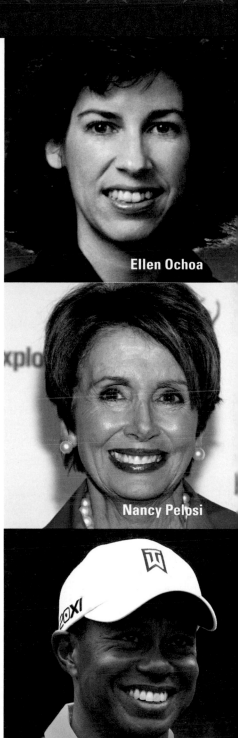

Ellen Ochoa

Nancy Pelosi

Tiger Woods

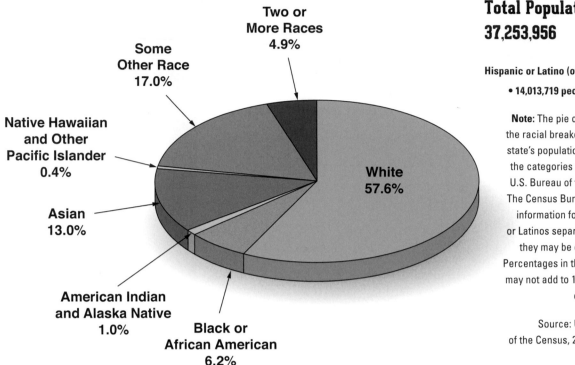

Two or
More Races
4.9%

Some
Other Race
17.0%

Native Hawaiian
and Other
Pacific Islander
0.4%

Asian
13.0%

American Indian
and Alaska Native
1.0%

Black or
African American
6.2%

White
57.6%

**Total Population
37,253,956**

Hispanic or Latino (of any race):
• 14,013,719 people (37.6%)

Note: The pie chart shows the racial breakdown of the state's population based on the categories used by the U.S. Bureau of the Census. The Census Bureau reports information for Hispanics or Latinos separately, since they may be of any race. Percentages in the pie chart may not add to 100 because of rounding.

Source: U.S. Bureau of the Census, 2010 Census

The Latino Face of California

Some cities are known for having a large population of a particular ethnic group. For example, Latinos make up almost half the population of Los Angeles. Most are from Mexico, but large numbers also come from, or have ancestors who came from, the Caribbean and Central and South America. But Latinos are not only in Los Angeles— their numbers are rising across the state. By 2020, California will have more Latinos than people with non-Hispanic European backgrounds.

Many California Latinos speak both English and Spanish. The state has celebrations every year during Hispanic Heritage Month, which runs from September 15 to October 15. Californians also celebrate Cinco de Mayo (which means "fifth of May" in Spanish) to honor the Mexican army's victory over French forces in 1862. Many places in California have Spanish names. For example, Los Angeles is Spanish for "the angels," and San Francisco is named after a Spanish mission that was named to honor St. Francis. The city of Fresno is named after the Spanish word for "ash tree." Even Alcatraz, the island in San Francisco Bay that houses a well-known former prison, has a Spanish name. Alcatraz is the Spanish word for "strange bird" or "pelican." Pelicans once lived on the island.

For many years, Californians with non-Hispanic European backgrounds had just about all the leadership roles in the state. Today, Mexican Americans and other Latinos are becoming more active in politics and business. In 1998, Cruz Bustamante was elected lieutenant governor, the second-highest position in the state government. He was the first Latino elected to a statewide government job in 120 years. Bustamante won reelection in 2002. Another **prominent** Latino politician is Antonio Villaraigosa, who was twice elected mayor of Los Angeles.

An Asian Influence

When the gold rush began, many Chinese people settled in cities and in small towns to farm, build the railroads, and work in mines. The Chinese and people from other Asian countries have had a lasting effect on California. For example, Japanese farmers helped turn the Central Valley into a rich agricultural area.

Life for Asian Americans, however, has not always been easy. Racism made it hard for the first Asians in California to find work. In the past, some Californians encouraged the U.S. government to pass laws to keep more Asians from moving to the United States. Many state laws also limited the legal rights of Chinese immigrants.

During World War II, the United States and its allies fought against Japan, Germany, and their allies. Many Americans feared that Japanese Americans would not be loyal to the United States. As a result, the U.S. government rounded up Japanese Americans and sent them to special detention facilities, called internment camps. These camps were like prisons. In 1944, the U.S. Supreme Court ruled that the U.S. government could not detain loyal citizens, and the camps were closed.

California today is home to many people who have roots in other countries in Asia. One out of every four Asian Americans in California is from the Philippines, about the same number as those who are Chinese American. Though the state still has a large Japanese American population, there are even more people today who trace their origins to Vietnam, India, or Korea. People from each Asian group celebrate different traditional holidays. For example, every year in late January or early February, Vietnamese Americans celebrate their New Year.

Dodger Jackie Robinson won Major League Baseball's Most Valuable Player Award in 1949.

In Fremont, Californians from India or whose ancestors are from India get together each year to celebrate their culture. Many women wear the traditional long garment called a sari, and everyone enjoys Indian music and food.

California's African Americans

African Americans have lived in California since Spanish and Mexican times. Many came during the gold rush. Some came as slaves with their owners. Other African Americans arrived as free people wanting to start a new life.

Slavery was outlawed in California even before it became a state. African Americans, however, still struggled with racism. They were not being treated the same as white Americans, and it made their lives more difficult.

Many African Americans came to California during and after World War II. They often lived in poor neighborhoods of big cities. Many African Americans also had trouble getting good jobs. Despite their struggles, African Americans from California have made important contributions to all areas of society. Baseball great Jackie Robinson grew up in Pasadena. In 1947, when he began playing for the Dodgers, he broke the color barrier that had kept African Americans out of Major League Baseball. In 1973, Los Angeles elected its first African-American mayor, Tom Bradley. He held the position for 20 years. Several other California cities have since elected black mayors.

Home Sweet California

One out of every eight people in the United States lives in California.

The First Californians Today

Before Europeans arrived, Native Americans were the only people in California. The Spanish brought diseases to California that killed many of the Natives. European and American settlers also pushed the Native people off their lands. Historians believe there were once at least 300,000 Native Americans in California. By the late 19th century, there were fewer than 30,000. However, numbers have risen since then. Today, more than 571,000 Californians identify themselves as Native American or part Native American. That is more than in any other state.

Many California Native Americans live on reservations set aside for their tribes. These people have their own governments and laws, but they are also U.S. citizens. Many people on the reservations face poverty, though some tribes have set up casinos to make money. Others make and sell traditional art.

Facing the Future

Ensuring that all Californians have equal rights and live together peacefully is one of the state's big challenges. In recent years, every ethnic group has faced problems during tough economic times. But for people from many parts of the world, California remains a land of opportunity. Eddie Medrano came to the state from Nicaragua. He struggled to find work, but he said, "I love your California. Over here, you work hard, but you enjoy life a little more." Many people agree that California is the place to be. As singer and voice actress Beth Anderson puts it, "Everything is just better in California - the wine, the food, fruits and vegetables, the comforts of living. Even the instrumentalists are generous and curious. Everything is wonderful."

California State Fair

Doo Dah Parade

July 4th Fireworks

1. California State Fair

Held in July, this fair in California's capital city, Sacramento, includes rides, horse races, food, and music from local and national singers and bands.

2. California Strawberry Festival in Oxnard

This festival is considered one of the top festivals in the country. It celebrates everything strawberry, and it features rides, music, crafts, and of course strawberries. Since the first festival in 1984, it has raised more than $4 million for various charities.

3. Doo Dah Parade in Pasadena

This April parade pokes fun at the more serious Tournament of Roses parade. Anyone can join in, and there are no rules. Marchers have included the Marching Martian Nannies and the Killer Clown Doctors from Outer Space.

4. July 4th Fireworks Spectacular in Hollywood

The Hollywood Bowl, a famous outdoor concert venue, holds a concert every July 4th followed by a large fireworks show. The Los Angeles Philharmonic plays, along with a famous singer each year.

5. Kite Party in Huntington Beach

At this festival held on the beach, kite fans of all ages can watch professional kite fliers, take kite lessons, and fly kites of their own.

6. Monterey Jazz Festival

Held every September, the longest-running jazz festival in the world features shopping, exhibits, and music by some of the world's most talented jazz musicians, including Tony Bennett, Diana Krall, and Harry Connick, Jr.

7. North Lake Tahoe SnowFest

The West's largest winter carnival takes place every February at this beautiful mountain resort. Activities include parades, fireworks, and music. There is also an ice cream eating contest, and some people even jump into the lake!

8. Old Town Cinco de Mayo

Cinco de Mayo is the 5th of May, a day when Mexicans celebrate their heritage and culture. In early May, the Old Town section of San Diego holds the largest Cinco de Mayo celebration north of Mexico, full of music, food, and dancing.

9. Renaissance Pleasure Faire

The largest Renaissance festival in southern California, the Renaissance Pleasure Faire celebrates Elizabethan life with music, sword fighting, parades, and knights on horseback.

10. Tournament of Roses Parade

Since 1890, Pasadena has hosted the Tournament of Roses parade on New Year's Day. Each colorful float is covered with roses, other flowers, and parts of plants. The parade is watched by hundreds of thousands of people along the parade route.

Monterey Jazz Festival

Renaissance Pleasure Faire

Tournament of Roses Parade

The Capitol in Sacramento has offices for the governor, lieutenant governor, and members of the state legislature.

How the Government Works

Running such a large state takes hard work from many people. California's towns and cities have governments that handle local affairs and pass local laws. As of 2010, the state had 482 cities and towns. Local citizens elect **councils** to run their cities and towns. Most cities also have mayors.

The towns and cities of California are located in 58 counties. In most counties, voters elect a board of supervisors. The supervisors act like business managers who try to do what is best for the county. Other county jobs include sheriff, county clerk, school **superintendent**, and district attorney. Voters elect people for all these positions. Some counties in California have "home rule." This means they can write documents called *charters*, which are like local constitutions. The charters give county officials more control over how their county is run. Dozens of cities in California also have home rule.

California's Lawmakers

The state legislature makes laws for all Californians. The state's lawmakers, or legislators, belong to one of two houses: the state assembly or the state senate. They are elected by the voters from their district. The assembly has 80 members, and the senate has 40. All California voters also elect the governor and some other major state officials.

This is the chamber in which the state assembly meets. The assembly proposes, analyzes, and debates over 6,000 bills in a two-year period.

Branches of Government

Executive

This branch includes the governor, lieutenant governor, secretary of state, treasurer, and attorney general. People who hold these offices are chosen in elections. The governor has a four-year term and can serve only two terms in a row. The governor appoints many other people who help run the government, and prepares a proposed budget every year. The governor and the legislature eventually have to agree on the final budget.

Legislative

The state assembly and state senate make up the legislative branch. Legislators propose and pass laws for the state. Members of the assembly can serve up to three terms of two years each. Senators can serve up to two terms of four years each.

Judicial

The courts are run by judges. They decide criminal or civil cases, often with the help of a jury. In criminal cases, people accused of a crime go on trial to determine whether

they are guilty. In civil cases, one person or group sues another, and the court then decides which side is right. Sometimes courts must also decide whether a certain law is legal under the California constitution. The judicial system includes different levels of courts. The loser in a case can appeal to a higher court. Some appeals are heard by the state's highest court, the California supreme court. The governor selects judges for the supreme court. However, voters must approve judges in the first regular election after they are appointed. They need to be approved again every twelve years.

California voters also elect people to represent them in the U.S. Congress. There are two houses of Congress, the Senate and the House of Representatives. Every state has two U.S. senators. In the House, the number of representatives from each state depends on the state's population. That number can change every ten years after the latest U.S census. In 2013, California had 53 representatives in the House. That is more than any other state, because California has the largest state population.

California residents take to the polls at a polling station during the 2012 Presidential Election.

Governor Jerry Brown shakes hands with a senator after signing the Safe and Responsible Driver Act, or Bill 60, into law.

How a Bill Becomes a Law

A bill, or proposed law, can be introduced by an assembly member or a senator. The bill first goes to a committee, which invites the public to comment on it. If the committee votes to approve the measure, the whole assembly or senate reviews the bill and debates its points. If one house of the legislature approves the bill, it goes to the other house. If the second house makes any changes to the bill, it must go back to the first house. In some cases, members from each house get together to make changes that both houses can agree upon. Most bills need only a majority vote to pass, but budget measures or bills that raise taxes must be approved by a two-thirds vote.

Once a bill is approved by both houses, it goes to the governor, who can either sign it into law or veto—reject—it. If the governor does not take any action on the bill, it becomes a law. If the governor vetoes the bill, it can still become a law if two-thirds of the members of both the state assembly and the state senate vote to override the veto.

Residents of California are very vocal about how the government's decisions affect them. Here California state workers are protesting a plan that would cut their salaries.

★ Dianne Feinstein: U.S. Senator, 1992-

Born in San Francisco, Dianne Feinstein became the first female mayor of the city in 1978. After balancing San Francisco's budget nine years in a row, *City and State* magazine named her the country's "Most Effective Mayor." Feinstein is now the oldest currently serving U.S. Senator, having served since 1992.

★ Richard Nixon: U.S. President, 1969-1974

Richard Nixon was born in Yorba Linda, California. Nixon was the 37th President of the United States. People involved in Nixon's re-election campaign broke into the Watergate Hotel in Washington, D.C. and stole information that would help his campaign. Nixon tried to keep it a secret, and when he was going to be impeached, or fired, he resigned instead.

★ Arnold Schwarzenegger: Governor, 2003-2011

Born in Austria in 1947, Arnold Schwarzenegger moved to California in 1968. He won 12 world bodybuilding titles, and he later starred in such Hollywood films as *Terminator* and *Kindergarten Cop*. In 2003, he was elected governor in a recall election that removed the former governor from office. In 2006, Schwarzenegger was elected to a second term.

CALIFORNIA ★ ★ ★
YOU CAN MAKE A DIFFERENCE

Contacting Lawmakers

You can use the Internet to help you find contact information for the state and local politicians who represent you. To find a California state representative, go to:

www.assembly.ca.gov

Click on "Find My Representative," and then type in your address and zip code in the boxes. You can find the same information at:

www.sen.ca.gov

Click "Find My Senator." Enter your home address, including zip code, to get contact information for your state senator and representative.

The Initiative Process

California has a process that lets citizens propose and pass laws and even make changes to the state's constitution. This is called the initiative process. California voters have passed initiative measures covering many issues, including taxes, term limits, and wildlife protection.

Everyone Can Take Part

At the local level, citizens have many ways to get involved in politics. They can serve on boards that oversee schools, libraries, and parks.

High school students in San Francisco elect their own representatives to the board of education. The student representatives help the school board learn more about issues that concern students.

People can also work to help candidates running for election to local or state office. In addition, citizens can work together to get an initiative on the ballot in local as well as statewide elections.

The Silver Lake Farmer's Market is held every Tuesday and Saturday. Local farmers sell fruits, vegetables, and flowers.

Making a Living

An economy consists of the value of the goods people make and the services they provide. The total value of goods and services produced in California is almost $2 trillion. That is more than 10 percent of all goods and services produced in the whole United States. No other state comes close to producing as much. If California were a separate country, it would have the eighth-largest economy in the world.

Tops in Farming

When Americans munch on almonds or walnuts, they are usually eating food that was grown in California. The state's farmers also grow almost all the artichokes, figs, olives, and clingstone peaches eaten in the United States. California farmers lead in the production of many other products—including milk, grapes, lettuce, strawberries, broccoli, lemons, carrots, celery, and alfalfa hay.

California is by far the number-one agricultural state in the country. Each year, its farms grow and sell crops, livestock, and other agricultural products worth well over $40 billion. These foods end up on kitchen tables around the globe. The Salinas Valley, one of the major farming regions in California, has been called the salad bowl of the world because of the many types of vegetables grown there.

Migrant workers are picking green beans.

To harvest crops, California farmers rely heavily on migrant workers. These workers travel to different farms when and where they are needed. Some come from Mexico each day to work and then return home at night. Others live in California, harvesting different crops at different times of the year. Many of the workers came across the border—to get work and earn money for their families—without having **obtained** the necessary U.S. government documents giving them the right to enter the country. These people are known as "undocumented" immigrants. U.S. law **prohibits** the hiring of undocumented workers, but many employers ignore the law. In some cases, employers pay undocumented workers lower wages than other workers. They also give them poorer working conditions, because employers know the undocumented laborers will not complain to government authorities. Migrant workers have difficult lives, and many Californians are working to improve the migrants' living and working conditions.

A big problem for California farming is finding enough water. Farms use the largest share of the state's total water consumption. In recent years, the demand for water by farmers and residents has grown, but the supply of water has not. The state has also suffered from periods of drought that have lasted for years. These dry weather conditions have helped cause many dangerous wildfires that destroy homes and crops.

Wealth from the Ground

Mining is very important in California. The state's miners dig up metals and rocks that are used to make products or building materials. These include sand and gravel used in construction and cement. California is the only state that produces boron, which is used to make some types of soap. The state also still mines gold, but not as much as in the past.

Californians drill deep below the earth and under the water offshore to take out petroleum and natural gas. California is one of the nation's top oil-producing and oil-refining states. It is also a leader in producing energy from renewable sources such as wind and solar power. The world's largest solar power plant is located in California's Mojave Desert. However, California must import most of the electricity it needs from other states. For this reason, and because of weather conditions and other factors, the state has had energy problems. In 2000 and 2001, the state experienced blackouts that left many people without electricity, and the price of electricity became very high.

Another important natural resource is timber. California has more forest land than any other state except Alaska. Most of the trees used for paper, lumber, and other wood products come from northern California. Some state residents want limits on cutting trees, since logging may destroy homes for rare wildlife and cause the erosion, or wearing away, of soil. Others argue that limits on logging may hurt lumber companies and cause a loss of jobs. About 5 million acres (2,023,428 ha) of California forest are suitable for harvest. Currently, about 22,000 acres (8,903 ha) are logged in the state. In September 2013, the U.S. House of Representatives approved a bill that would expand logging in California's national forests. Many believe that extra timber is fuel for wildfires, and logging would help keep communities safer.

10 KEY INDUSTRIES

Aerospace

Computers

Engineering

1. Aerospace

Aerospace is the business of putting humans and machinery in Earth's atmosphere and outer space. Many companies in California produce and sell parts and equipment that make this possible.

2. Agriculture

California has more than 80,000 farms. Agriculture brings the state over $44 billion a year, making it one of the leading industries there.

3. Computers

Silicon Valley, near San Jose, is considered the computer capital of the world. Many Internet-based companies and companies that produce microchips, hardware, and software call that area home.

4. Engineering

Different types of engineers in California do everything from building and fixing bridges and interstates to designing machinery and building computers.

5. Entertainment

Hollywood is the movie-making capital of the world. Not only are movies, TV shows, and music albums made there, but many Hollywood stars live in Los Angeles and its surrounding communities.

CALIFORNIA

6. Healthcare

With more than 300,000 registered nurses licensed in the state, nursing is the largest healthcare profession in California. Other healthcare-related professions are growing, too, such as doctors and home-health aides.

7. Mining

With its gold mining history, it is no surprise that California is still one of the largest producers of gold. Other mined products include oil, boron, and gypsum.

8. Real Estate

The most populated state in the United States must keep up with demand. Californians love their real estate, and some of the most beautiful (and expensive) homes can be found there, making it a big business.

9. Retail

Big cities such as Los Angeles and San Francisco are known for their great shopping. Both residents and visitors to California love to shop, which makes the retail profession one of the largest in the state.

10. Telecommunications

Telecommunications is the science and technology of sending messages through phones, radios, televisions, and computers. California is at the center of this technology.

Healthcare

Real Estate

Retail

Recipe for Grape Tarts

Grapes earned California over $4 billion in 2012, making it the second most valuable crop in the state. With the help of an adult, follow this recipe to make a dessert that highlights the grape!

What You Need

All-purpose flour, for work surface

1/2 package frozen puff pastry, thawed

1 large egg yolk

1 tablespoon (15 ml) heavy cream

2 cups (128 g) red seedless grapes

2 tablespoons (25 g) granulated sugar

Pinch of salt

Brown sugar, for sprinkling

What to Do

• Preheat oven to 400°F (200°C).

• On a lightly floured work surface, unfold pastry.

• Cut 4 circles using the rim of a glass. Transfer to a baking sheet and refrigerate until firm, about 15 minutes.

• Whisk together egg yolk and cream; set egg wash aside.

• Toss together grapes, granulated sugar, and salt in a medium bowl.

• Divide grape mixture among tart shells, keeping it inside the borders.

• Brush edges of tarts with egg wash, and sprinkle with brown sugar.

• Bake 23-27 minutes or until pastry is crisp and golden and grapes start to collapse.

• Let cool on a wire rack.

Sales of the iPhone have made Apple one of the most valuable companies in the world.

Making Things Happen

When people in foreign countries buy a product made in America, there is a good chance the item came from California. The state exports more goods than any other state. These include cars, processed foods, and dozens of other products. California is also a leader in the aerospace industry. Aerospace companies make airplanes and spacecraft. Californians still make much of the equipment that sends people into space or flies them across the country and around the world.

Creative Companies

BoxCycle is a San Francisco-based company that provides a website with which you can buy and sell used boxes.

The Digital World

The area around San Jose is known as Silicon Valley. Silicon is a material used to make computer chips. The area has many companies that make computer hardware and software. Apple is one of many such companies based there. Silicon Valley and San

Children ride the King Arthur Carrousel at Disneyland Park in Anaheim.

Francisco are also home to many of the biggest Internet companies. Google and Yahoo! have headquarters there, as do eBay and the social-networking site Facebook.

At Your Service

The largest part of California's economy is the service industry. This includes such businesses as hotels, restaurants, banks and other financial institutions, retail stores, and insurance companies. Hospitals and schools are also part of the service sector. Two other important industries in California are tourism and film production.

Tourism adds close to $100 billion to the state's economy each year. People from all over the world come to explore Los Angeles, San Francisco, and other cities. Animal lovers flock to the San Diego Zoo, one of the most famous zoos in the world. Nature enthusiasts enjoy the natural beauty of Yosemite, Redwood, Sequoia, and California's five other national parks. Visitors are also attracted to the state's scenic coastline and sandy beaches. Disneyland and other well-known theme parks attract fun-loving visitors of all ages.

Filmmakers create movies and television shows. Los Angeles is the center of the film-production industry. Entertainment companies have studios in the region, where they film movies and TV shows. The entertainment industry alone brings in more than $33 billion.

Education

Education is very important in California—and a big part of the economy. California has more than 10,000 public elementary and secondary schools, with more than 300,000 teachers and more than 6.2 million students—more than any other state.

California is also noted for its system of public colleges and universities. The University of California has 10 campuses around the state, including UC Berkeley and UCLA. In addition, the California State University system has 23 campuses, including Cal State Fullerton and Fresno State. California has a large network of community colleges as well.

California is also home to many fine private colleges and universities, such as Stanford University and the California Institute of Technology (Caltech). The University of Southern California, or USC, is another well-known private university. It has long been a rival school to its crosstown neighbor, UCLA.

Challenges for the Economy

The state was hard hit by the recession, or economic downturn, that affected the whole country by 2008. State and local governments in California had a difficult time balancing their budgets and paying for education and other services for a growing population. Home values fell sharply, while the unemployment rate soared. In December 2009, more than 12 percent of workers were out of a job. That was higher than the national average of 10 percent for that month. During 2009, more than 579,000 workers in California lost their jobs.

Californians face big problems in reviving and expanding their economy. They must also work to protect the environment as the population grows. However, California has a skilled workforce and is rich in natural resources. The state has long been a leader in developing cutting-edge technology in nearly every field. It has more "green" jobs than any other state—a good sign for the state's future. Even in tough times, the people of California continue to enjoy their beautiful state and dream of a **prosperous** future.

CALIFORNIA
STATE MAP

Point St. George
KLAMATH R.
Modoc National Forest
Goose Lake
WARNER MTS.
101
97
KLAMATH
Redwood National Park
MOUNTAINS
Pit R.
395
Eureka
Shasta Lake
CASCADE RANGE
Cape Mendocino
Redding
Lassen Volcanic National Park
Punta Gorda
COAST
Eel R.
Chico
Plumas National Forest
Sacramento R.
Mendocino National Forest
SACRAMENTO VALLEY
Yuba City
Truckee
80
Lake Tahoe
Santa Rosa
Marshall Gold Discovery State Historic Park
Eldorado National Forest
SIERRA
50
101
80
Sacramento
395
Point Reyes
5
Stockton
Tuolumne R.
Mono Lake
Berkeley
Oakland
Fremont
Modesto
Yosemite National Park
6
San Francisco
San Francisco Bay
San Jose
SAN JOAQUIN R.
DIABLO RANGE
NEVADA
Owens R.
INYO MOUNTAINS
AMARGOSA RANGE
DEATH VALLEY
Death Valley National Park
Santa Cruz
Monterey Bay
Santa Cruz
Monterey
Salinas
SANTA CRUZ MTS.
SANTA LUCIA RANGE
Salinas R.
Kings Canyon National Park
Fresno
Kings R.
Mount Whitney
PANAMINT RANGE
PACIFIC
SAN JOAQUIN VALLEY
5
San Luis Obispo
Bakersfield
395
MOJAVE
OCEAN
Los Padres National Forest
Edwards Air Force Base
Mojave National Preserve
DESERT
15
Barstow
40
Needles
Point Conception
101
SANTA YNEZ MTS.
Santa Clarita
Palmdale
Santa Barbara
Oxnard
SAN GABRIEL MTS.
SAN BERNARDINO MTS.
95
San Miguel
Santa Barbara Chan.
Glendale
Joshua Tree National Park
Santa Rosa
Santa Cruz
Los Angeles
10
San Bernardino
Channel Islands National Park
Long Beach
Anaheim
Riverside
10
Blythe
Disneyland
Santa Ana
Colorado R.
CHANNEL
Irvine
Cleveland National Forest
Salton Sea
SONORAN
Santa Catalina
15
DESERT
Anza-Borrego Desert State Park
San Nicolas
ISLANDS
Gulf of
Oceanside
Escondido
Cleveland National Forest
San Clemente
Santa Catalina
5
San Diego
8
El Centro
Chula Vista

PACIFIC OCEAN

Legend

	Interstate
	Major Highway
●	City or Town
★	State Capital

▲	Highest Point in State
▲	Mountains
★	Historic Site
🌲	National Forest

🌲	State Forest
🏛	National Park
	State Park
■	Other Points of Interest

N
W E
S

0   miles   150

CALIFORNIA ★ ★ ★
MAP SKILLS

1. What is the southernmost Channel Island?

2. What major highway runs north-south along the western edge of the state?

3. What is the highest peak in California? Which mountain range is it part of?

4. What historic site is located outside the state capital?

5. How many national parks can you find on this map?

6. What is the state's northernmost lake?

7. What two mountain ranges surround Death Valley?

8. Which interstate would you take from Los Angeles to Blythe?

9. What point of interest is located near Palmdale?

10. Which mountains are south of San Francisco?

Monterey Bay

Los Padres National Forest

Mojave National Preserve

10. Santa Cruz Mountains
9. Edwards Airforce Base
8. 10
7. Panamint Range and Amagosa Range
6. Goose Lake
5. 8
4. Marshall Gold Discovery State Historic Park
3. Mount Whitney, Sierra Nevada
2. 101
1. San Clemente Island

State Seal, Flag, and Song

California's official state seal was adopted in 1849 at the convention that decided on the state's constitution. The seal shows Minerva, the Roman goddess of wisdom, with a grizzly bear at her feet. The seal also shows a miner at work near the Sacramento River. The peaks of the Sierra Nevada are shown in the distance. The state seal includes the word "Eureka," which means "I have found it" in Greek. That refers to the discovery of gold in California. The 31 stars near the top edge of the seal are a reminder that California was soon to become the 31st state.

California's flag is based on the flag used during the Bear Flag Revolt in 1846. During this revolt, settlers took over a fort in Sonoma and declared California an independent republic that would not be controlled by Mexico. The grizzly bear represents strength, and the red star is a reference to the lone star of Texas. The original bear flag flew over the fort from mid-June to early July of 1846. It became the official state flag in 1911.

To see the lyrics of the California State Song, "I Love You, California," go to
www.statesymbolsusa.org/California/CA_StateSong.html

Glossary

budget   An official statement from a government about how much money it plans to spend during a particular period of time and how it will pay for what it needs.

confrontations   Situations in which people or groups fight or challenge each other in an angry way.

councils   Groups of people who are chosen to make rules, laws, or decisions about something.

debris   The pieces that are left after something has been destroyed.

fable   A short story that is meant to teach the reader a lesson.

immigrants   People who come to a country to live there.

invested   Committed money in order to earn a financial return.

irrigation   The watering of land by artificial means to foster plant or crop growth.

legal   Of or relating to the law.

menaced   Showed a plan to bring upon harm.

missions   Places that are dependent on a larger religious organization for direction or financial support.

obtained   Gained usually by planned action or effort.

prohibits   Prevents from doing something.

prominent   Important or well known.

prosperous   Marked by success or well-being.

silicon   A chemical element that is found in the Earth's crust and is used in computers and electronics.

superintendent   A person who directs or manages a place, department, or organization.

More About California

BOOKS

Duffield, Katy S. *California History for Kids: Missions, Miners, and Moviemakers in the Golden State*. Chicago, IL: Chicago Review Press, 2012.

Holub, Joan. *What Was the Gold Rush?* New York, NY: Grosset and Dunlap, 2013.

Orr, Tamra B. *California*. New York, NY: Scholastic, 2011.

Sonneborn, Liz. *California Indians*. Portsmouth, NH: Heinemann, 2011.

Weber, Matt. *San Francisco: The Alphabet Book: An A to Z Journey Through San Francisco's Sights and History*. Chicago, IL: 121 Publications, 2011.

WEBSITES

California History and Government for Kids:

www.ca.gov/HomeFamily/ChildrenFamilies/JustforKids/History.html

California State Capitol Museum:

capitolmuseum.ca.gov/kids/kids_home_flash.html

California Travel and Tourism Commission:

www.visitcalifornia.com

ABOUT THE AUTHORS

Michael Burgan is the author of more than two hundred books for children and young adults, both fiction and nonfiction. His other books for Marshall Cavendish Benchmark include *The Lakota* and *The Arapaho* in the First Americans series; *Hiroshima: Birth of the Nuclear Age* in the Perspectives On series; and *Bat Researcher* in the Dirty and Dangerous Jobs series. A graduate of the University of Connecticut with a B.A. in history, Burgan is also a produced playwright. He lives with his wife, Samantha, in Connecticut.

William McGeveran is a longtime reference book editor and was editorial director at World Almanac Books, where he managed the development of *The World Almanac and Book of Facts*, *The World Almanac for Kids*, and *The World Almanac Book of Records*. Now a freelance writer and an editor, he has written and edited articles on current events and other topics for an online encyclopedia and other reference works. Bill and his wife have four grown children.

Index

Index